ISBN 978-1-173408-0-9:

Printed in the United States of America

Bradley Troutman

5443 Diane Avenue

Owensboro, Kentucky. 42301

About the Author

Bradley Troutman has been married to his best friend, Janie, for nearly forty years. They have four adult children, a Godly son-in-law, as well as a beautiful Granddaughter. Bradley and Janie have worked in various positions as lay people over the years at three different churches.

We would like to thank all those people along the way that God put in our life to make it better. We hope that the experiences shared in this book will bring you to a closer walk with God.

The purpose of this book is to help you see and recognize how God is at work in your life. To build a testimony of miracles, small and large, that have occurred in your life. Last but certainly not least, encourage you to share your testimony every chance you get.

A special thanks to my two sisters Kathy and Shannon for their encouragement and help with getting this message out to all who need to recognize how God is at work in their lives. Thank you to my friends Lois and Susann, who put so much effort into helping me with grammar, spelling, and all those English things I should have learned in eighth grade.

Table of Contents

Introduction

Grace is defined as the free and unmerited favor of God as manifested in the salvation of sinners and the bestowal of blessings. I am hoping to show you in the following pages that grace is so much more than you have ever imagined.

We are taught that grace is God's free gift to those of us who believe in Him. We are taught that we can't earn our way into heaven and our salvation is based on faith and no kind of work can earn your entrance into Heaven.

I will say I have to agree with that, but it doesn't stop with entrance into heaven. Once you have been what many Christians call, "saved," then you are an adopted child into the kingdom. God sends His Holy Spirit to live inside your soul. Those of you that have been filled with that Spirit know what I am talking about. This book is really more for you than those who have not yet accepted that free gift of grace. I hope to share some scriptures with you and some stories that prove beyond a shadow of a doubt that grace is so much more than forgiveness of your sins.

I hope to help you examine your personal walk with God and to help you to enrich that relationship. God doesn't want you to be a religion, He wants a relationship with you. A relationship is an interaction between more than one person. In this case, one person and one God. There is so much more to that relationship than most people can understand. The best way to explain it is in an old song we used to sing in church called "Bond of Love." It goes like this: "We are one in the bond of love. We are one in the bond of love. We have joined our spirits with the Spirit of God. We are one in the bond of love."

That means in this relationship you have with God, through His Spirit, you have a relationship with other believers. Yes, someone half way across the world feels the same spirit in their soul as you feel in your soul right here. Think back to how many times you have felt that unexplainable feeling you know is God. You get goose pimples, you weep uncontrollably, sometimes, you shout, you clap, you sing. When you get that Spirit in you it is like what Jesus said, "If the people don't shout out that I am Lord, then the rocks would." His Spirit is just so powerful.

Now if you know that feeling I am telling you about, then I want you to learn to experience the grace that is so much more than just forgiveness.

Chapter One

Grace is Deliverance

Scripture: 2nd Kings 6:17-20

Key Verse "Open his eyes, Lord, so that he may see."

In this story, Elisha's servant was worried about all the soldiers that had been sent to kill the prophet. When the servant went outside early in the morning, he could see they were surrounded by a whole army of soldiers with horses and chariots. They were ready to kill the whole town of Dothan, if that is what it took to bring Elisha to the king of Aram.

Now this servant had been with Elisha for a while and I am sure he had seen some amazing things happen. The king wanted Elisha captured because every time the king's army would make a move to sneak up on the nation of Israel's army, they would be warned by God through Elisha. The servant had to have seen what God was doing. Just recently, he had witnessed an axe head float to the surface of a creek just so the guy who borrowed it could return it to the owner.

Here is a lesson: God was protecting Elisha from the big things that come up in life. I mean, he had an army that was described as "a strong force" that was pursuing him. God was also taking care of the simple things that we tend to think He would not even care about. Elisha knew He cared.

God is the same way in our life too. He cares about the simple things in our life as much as He does if the army was at the door. Sometimes we need to open our eyes to see what God is doing in our life. Record those things in our memory to be part of our testimony to others how God is at work in our life.

I was a twenty-one-year-old man that had just graduated from tech school and went to work at a factory about fifty miles from my hometown. I was pretty much the average guy my age; I drank a little, I smoked a little and I was always on the lookout for something fun to do. I had never been with a woman in the biblical way, and was pretty naive when it came to the real world. I landed a really good job as an electronic technician in a manufacturing facility, I bought the sharpest Jeep CJ5 in our area and I was just beginning to enjoy my new-found freedom from home and school.

That is when the army of bad things began to surround my life. A girl I worked with was going through a divorce, and in order to make her soon-to-be ex-husband jealous, she wanted to date the guy with the best looking four-wheel drive vehicle in town. That was me. I know now that she was way more interested in my Jeep than me. This relationship was my first intimate encounter and I fell head over heels in love. "Young and dumb," I would call it now. To make a real long story short, conflict developed between me and her ex-husband. She ended up with child, not knowing for sure who was the father.

I had been out of church since my late teens, but I knew God from an earlier encounter. When I was thirteen years old my mom and dad divorced. A lady next door to us began to take me and my sister to a small Pentecostal church she was a member of that was close to our house. That is where I really was saved and really met God.

For a couple of years, our small group of youth would go to revivals to sing and worship with fellow believers all across the tri-state area where we lived. God's Holy Spirit was really alive in that group of believers. I recall telling our pastor I felt like God was calling me to preach. That was at age fourteen. Hard to believe that by age twenty two, I had found myself in such a spot.

I did something then that I had not done, unless I was really scared, and that was to pray. I had no knowledge of what God wanted to do with my life. I can look back now through all the years and realize that He would have done so much more if I had just asked. Best I can remember. I just said, "God, I know you are real and I need your help." I went to a church that next Sunday that I had never been to before, but I knew that is where I should start. I don't remember what denomination the church was or if I could even find it today. I went in not knowing anyone at all in the church. I am not sure if I was nervous about that beforehand; the important thing was I went in to meet God, and He was waiting there for me.

I have no idea of this pastor's name and I don't know how he prepared for his sermon that week. I do know that somehow God had written what that preacher said just for me. I cried when it came time for the invitation hymn. I met briefly with the pastor to set up a meeting the next week to discuss my situation. On my way back to my apartment, I stopped and purchased a Sunday paper from a local big city, like I did every Sunday. In the classified section of the paper that week was an employment ad for an electrician. I was not an electrician but a technician. I was more into the electronics part of the job than the wire up the switch part of the job and I had no experience at all as an electrician, but I applied anyway.

I had worked at the factory where this job was located for the one summer as just a "do whatever" type of guy; sweep, shovel, any type of dirty work the other union factory workers did not want to do. The plant manager's son and I were fishing buddies and he worked there that summer also. God was lining up this electrical job up for me three years before I needed it, and I had no idea. I wasn't even wanting to be an electrician I wanted to be a lawyer at that time. I filled out an application, and even though I had no experience as an electrician, they offered me the job.

This may not sound like much to some people, but I knew God had done this just for me. You would have thought after seeing that happen, I would have just jumped at the opportunity to fellowship with a God who I had abandoned for all those years. But, I did not. Looking back now it would have hurt my feelings if I had done that for someone and then they just ignored me for a while. That is what I did to God. A new job back in my home town with my family, never giving God the thanks or the credit He deserved, yet He still loved me.

That is just a part of what grace can do. I did not deserve to get a new job, I had sinned. I did not deserve to be relocated closer to my family, I had sinned. I did nothing on my own except to humble myself before He who is on the throne. We are all sinners and can be saved by God's grace. What you do after receiving this grace is unlimited if you will trust God with your life decisions.

Deliverance is just one part of God's grace. That is not all of what God has for you either. He will keep you from putting yourself into situations like I had found myself in, if you will heed the warning signs He places before you. You remember that sharp Jeep I told you about earlier. He tried to keep me from going back to see this woman the first night I went to her house. She lived on a gravel road up on top of a hill. When I left her house, I was so excited about my new found relationship with her that I must have gunned the engine a little too much and my sharp looking Jeep ran just enough off the road to put a big scratch on the side, marred forever. God was telling me, "Stay away from this girl." Have I mentioned I was young and dumb at the time? On that night, if I had been walking as close to God as I should have been, I would have never gone back to her house. Before God delivered me from that town, I had my tires slashed, my Jeep's canvas top sliced, and my heart broken. I was blind to the signs He had given me.

Two weeks from the time I had asked God to deliver me from the situation that I was in, I was working in a job that I had no qualifications for, living back in the security of my mother's home. I never told Him thanks until now, "Thanks, God."

1. Have you ever been in a situation where you thought there was no hope?
   Read Acts 12: 1-19
   Write your answer here.

2. Do you realize this is part of your testimony?   Yes or No.

3. Would you consider this a miracle in your life? Make some notes below about your story. Would you be willing to share your story? Who would you like to share your story with?

Chapter Two

Grace is Rescuing.

Scripture: John 3:16 *For God so loved the world that He gave His only begotten Son, so that whosever believe in Him would have everlasting life.*

For thirty six years, almost thirty seven years, I have been married to my wife and best friend, Janie. Her name is Jane, but she prefers Janie. My first experience with a woman sure didn't work out very well. This one has lasted quite a bit longer. God has given me the woman with the most beautiful heart on earth. When the writer of Proverbs wrote Chapter 31 verses 10 through 31, it was Janie he was talking about. Well at least verse 10 and verse 30 described her. I am sure there are more good women out there in the world, but the one God picked for me was a perfect fit.

"It was getting kind of late one early October night." That was the first line of the song I wrote about her after we met. It was on a Thursday night. The biggest yearly event in town was going on that week with rides, food booths, games and such. I had gone down there with my friend James. We were just out doing guy stuff and we were going to play pinball at a local establishment when we left the festival.

"If you see Shellie, then we have to avoid her. She wanted to come down here with me tonight, but I told her I was busy," James said.

The only problem is that my vision was probably 20/100 or worse. Well, in that crowd of over a thousand people squeezed into a three block area, we ran right square into his girlfriend, Shellie. With Shellie was an 18 year old girl with a mischievous smirk and long blonde hair. She walked right up to me and took her right hand and slapped my ball cap right off my head. It was a white and blue hat that matched my flannel shirt perfectly. I think I caught it before it actually hit the ground, I was always pretty athletic.

She said, "Shellie said your hair was thinning and you were self-conscience about it and I was just checking it out." That was the beginning of a wonderful relationship that will endure for an eternity. Yes, I have lost most of my hair since then, and she is still here.

We were engaged in December and married the following May. This was a rescue for me, and yet, God did this for me even though I was still just a wandering sinner who had been saved in his teens. God had a plan for me, and Janie was her name.

Friday afternoon May the 21, it was less than twenty-four hours before our wedding. The rehearsal was to begin at seven o'clock and the church was about thirty-five minutes from where I cross the river that runs between her state and mine. I am still driving that Jeep that the bank and I own. About two blocks from the bridge my temperature gauge on the instrument panel had peaked and smoke was pouring out from my engine compartment. This was ten years before cell phones. There was a pay phone on the corner, but I had nobody to call since they were all on their way to the rehearsal or at the rehearsal. That is, except my brother, Mark. Mark was running late for some reason that I don't remember, but I do know why. God knew that my Jeep was going to overheat, and Mark was the only way He could get me there. There was no doubt in my mind, then or now, this was an intervention from God.

That was a rescue, but that was not "THE" rescue. Janie and I were just getting to know each better. We had fallen head over heels in love and that was about the extent of the knowledge we had of each other. She was of a different religion than I was, and her mom was more worried about that than I was. Again, I was not walking with God like I should have been, or I would have put my foot down when we had to take marriage classes at her church for six weeks to check our compatibility. The compatibility test was fine; what bothered me was they said we would have to swear to raise our children to be that religion.

I told Janie I did not agree with that, I would sign it, but only so we could get married. She was starry-eyed in love with me and she assured me that we would do what I said, "Wow," she does fit into more than just verse 10 and 31 of Proverbs 31 still to this day.

After we had married, we lived in my hometown about thirty miles away from her mom and dad. The first year and longer we went over their house on Saturday nights. We would get there around 4:30 in the afternoon. Her dad would get home about 5:00. We would go to their church service that was at 5:30 then be back to their house by 6:30 to eat the most awful chili I had ever eaten, and burgers that had cooked in the oven while we were at church. Now that is love! I never got used to those burgers or those church services. I knew the real God, and I hate to say it, but He was not there.

As we were approaching our first anniversary, we really had no friends except her mom and dad. My sister's church had a softball team looking for players and my brother in-law knew that I was a good ball player and that Janie, and I weren't going to church in our town, so they invited me to join the team. You could have two non-church members on the team. It was a good outreach tool for churches looking to reach the lost. Since Janie and I went to church on Saturday night with her mom and dad, there was no reason we couldn't go to a Sunday morning church service. The ball players were supposed to attend at least once a month, and Sunday School would count.

After we got to spend some time with the ball team and visited the church a few times the people actually got to know us by name. We had gone to church with her mom and dad for over a year and I did not know one single person outside of family. The only thing I knew was the priest was the guy who sent a keg of beer over to our reception as a gift from the church. My dad was more than a little bit upset. Dad was no saint, but in my twenty years at home there was never an ounce of alcohol in our house.

The church had a new pastor that my sister just bragged about. He was an older fellow probably sixty, well at that time in my life sixty was older. He was a "Fire and Brimstone" Southern Baptist preacher. It was like a revival service every week. Janie and I joined a couple's Sunday School class and were even attending some Sunday nights. Janie had been in church all her life, from infant baptism through high school. She was not dedicated to the church as much as she was doing the right thing to please her mother. That would be known as works, by the way. She had learned all the head knowledge about God; more than most of the people that I had ever gone to church with. The thing she was lacking was the fact she had never invited Jesus into her heart. That is what God wants. He wants to write His words on your heart.

One night there came a knock on our door. It was the preacher and one of the guys on the ball team and they asked if they could come in. They came in and sat on the couch and just chit-chatted for a while, then the preacher asked about our relationship with God. I told them I was saved when Kathy, my sister, was saved a long time ago, and I did believe in God. When they asked Janie, she began to tear up and could hardly speak.

Brother Pruden ask her if she would like to invite Jesus into her heart and she did. We all got those goose pimples and cried. Janie called my sister and told her on the phone what had happened, that she had been saved.

There is the rescue right there. How long had God planned to reach out to this young woman and give her an opportunity to surrender to Him. He could see inside her heart and now, His spirit was living in her soul. That was the rescue.

1. When an unexpected opportunity comes your way, do you think God may have placed you there?

2. Have you ever considered that it may have been Divine intervention? Read John 3:15-18. Do you realize that you have eternal life? When you became born again, God sent his Holy Spirit to dwell within your soul.

3. Write about your salvation experience. Think of ways your experience could help others that have not surrendered their hearts to God.

Chapter Three

Grace is Comforting

Scripture: John 11: 35 Jesus wept

Janie and I had become regular members at the church and we were there any time the doors were opened. Her, a newborn Christian and me, just a sinner saved by grace. The excitement in that little church was something only God could do. Sunday school attendance was running around eighty five every Sunday when Janie and I joined the church. Before we left the church had grown to over two hundred.

Janie and I had a daughter in the fall of 1984. We named her Dustaniel Marie. Janie said I could name the baby if it was a girl and she would name the baby if the baby was a boy. There is a story or two about her later in this book.

When Dusti was around two years old, Janie became pregnant again. We had agreed we would like to have three or four children, so we were very excited to learn about the upcoming event. As I mentioned before, we were regular members to every event that church had going from to Bible Study to a visitation program that any church in the world would love to have today.

One Thursday, Janie informed me that she was having some pain and that she was spotting blood a little. She went to her doctor and he informed us that the baby had passed. I just want to say that only a real living God could have done what happened that day.

When they informed us at the doctor's office the baby had passed away, we were shaken up pretty bad, but to the doctor's office it was no more than a procedure. She would have to report the next day for an outpatient procedure. It was probably four or five o'clock in the evening when we arrived home. Janie called her mom and they cried on the phone. Her sister even came down to our town later that night to spend the night.

On a normal Thursday evening, we would have been at church for weekly visitation. Tonight, we were just going to stay home. I told you earlier how good the program was; let me explain more. Anywhere from twenty five to forty people would meet at the church at six thirty, some would take cards from visitors at last week's service and visit them. Some would take prospect cards we kept on file and visit, and others would stay behind and pray or watch the children. After the ones out visiting returned, we would share our visit stories, good or bad.

It was about seven o'clock when there was a knock on our front door. It was our deacon Bobby and his wife Debbie. Nobody knew about our loss except the doctor, Janie's sister, mom and dad and God. When I answered the door, I must have looked a little surprised to see them and then Bobby said, "I don't know why we are here Bradley. We set out to visit someone else, but it was like God said 'Stop here.'"

We shared the story of our loss that we had found out about earlier in the day. We hugged, we cried, we prayed. There is no doubt in my mind that night, the God of the Universe sent someone to our door to comfort two young adults that were hurting. Thank You God.

When Jesus approached the town of Bethany, Lazarus had already passed away. Martha, one of Lazarus's sisters, came to Jesus and said, "Lord if you had been here, he would have not died."

Then Jesus stated, "Your brother will live." Then her sister Mary came to Jesus and she said basically the same thing.

When Jesus saw her crying and how hurt she was, the Bible says that "Jesus wept". God saw how hurt Janie and I were for this loss. He sent someone by our house that night and we wept, and I am sure He did too. Bobby and Debbie went back and shared the news with the ones gathered at church for visitation. They told them all about our loss. It felt like God had divided our sorrow by every member that came to comfort us.

1. Have you ever experienced a loss in your life that really saddened you?

2. How did you get through this time, or have you? Read Psalm 147:3. and read John 14:15-21 You have that same Spirit these scriptures mention. "The Advocate" in some translations.

3. Make some notes here on some experiences you have had, where you prayed for comfort, and God sent just the right person, song, or something to comfort your pain.

Chapter Four

Grace is Unseen Protection

Scripture: John 10:10b *"I have come that they may have life more abundantly."*

After losing a baby, a young couple like us could have very well turned away from God, if not what He had done for us that night. Seeing how He comforted us in our time of sorrow with His Spirit that was living inside us, along with using other believers to help us, strengthened our faith. Janie and I began to serve more and more in the church. Janie was working in the preschool where our daughter Dusti, at seven days old, made her first appearance at Wing Avenue Baptist Church. I was teaching first and second grade boys and girls. Janie was in the nursery with Dusti. Janie wouldn't leave the preschool department until we were called to serve in another church.

My brother Mark had married a girl with two sons from another marriage. My sister Kathy, had invited Mark and his wife, Darlene, to that same church. Every week Darlene would say, "When are you going to let Dusti come out and spend the day with me?"

We would always have a reason not to let her go out there and spend the day. We were very protective of Dusti, she was our only little girl. One day, we gave in. I can't remember what we were doing that would make us do that, but she was four and half years old and we just gave in.

When we returned to my brother's house, we entered the side door from the driveway into the kitchen. There was Mark's wife Darlene drying Dusti off with a towel.

Looking out from their kitchen window into the backyard, you could see a beautifully landscaped yard including a fish pond, that was probably three feet wide by six feet long and forty eight inches deep. The pond had gold fish and a few other species of reptiles living in or around the pond. The fish pond, that our less than forty eight inch tall daughter had just fallen into about five minutes before we returned. Darlene had just come into the house. She left Dusti for just a second to get something from the kitchen and when she looked outside that window, there was Dusti, somehow coming out of that pond. The side of this pond was straight up and down; she was shorter than the pond was deep, and she could not swim. How did she get out? I can't answer that, but I can tell you why.

Janie and I were walking as close to God as we could. It was an unexplainable relationship that we three shared. I wish I could say that it stayed that way. I firmly believe that there are unseen things that happen because of God. When God promised a life more abundantly, He meant it to include every part of your life, including your family. We don't understand why God doesn't intervene every time. I believe this time it was because God knew that our lives would be more abundant with Dusti. He was right.

When Jesus shared this scripture with the crowd, and the Pharisees, He was trying to explain to them what God would be to them if they would just accept the fact God was trying to save them. God had provided the sacrifice for their sins and from now on, their salvation was from His grace and not by works. Jesus warned believers there would be many that tried to lead them astray. The reason He had come was so that the sheep could have a better life. The key is two things: they are His sheep, and they hear His voice.

I want to stop here and tell you that to be one of His sheep is not that hard to do. When I taught grade school children in Sunday school, we would tell them it is as easy as A B C   .

The "A" is to accept that you are a sinner, but that doesn't mean you are a bad person. You really have no choice. I remember when I was four years old, I sinned and didn't even think twice about it as a four year old.

Mom left my sister Kathy and me home alone, while she went next door to visit our neighbor one day. There was an intercom system between the houses for some reason and of course a four and five year old would not know that mom could hear everything going on at our house while she was next door. Kathy, I am sure, decided we should walk down to this little neighborhood store that sold a variety of things. One of them was candy, and we should go down there and get some. We had no idea how to buy the candy, but Kathy said they would take bottle caps for candy. Boy, that was great. We could find fifteen or twenty of those just walking down the street to the store. Neither one of us could count to twenty, but we had a bunch. We went in the store, I think it was named "Mary's," we put our bottle caps up on the counter and asked how much candy we could get with this many bottle caps. You have never seen two more disappointed kids.

Kathy had a backup plan. Mom and Dad kept pennies on the coffee table in some kind of container that must not have been childproof. She figured that if we took some of those pennies to the store, we could get the candy. So, we filled our pants pockets full of pennies and sashayed on down to the little store, bought our fill of candy and headed home.

I am pretty sure we were surprised when we went in the front door and there was mom holding a belt. I learned more about the consequences of sin that day. Four years old stealing pennies, it's not your fault you are a sinner, but you are one.

The "B" is to believe in your heart that God loved you enough to send His Son for our sacrifice. That is His plan for us, yours, mine, and everyone's salvation. In Jeremiah, Chapter 31 God tells the prophet He will write His word on our heart and no longer would we be bound by the old law but there would be a new covenant to take the place of the old. It would be a personal relationship with each individual.

The "C" is for confess. That simply means tell God you know you are lost without Him. It can be a simple prayer like "God, I know I am a sinner. I know You loved me enough to send Jesus to be my sacrifice for sin. I want to ask You to come and write Your words on my heart, so I can have a relationship with You." Then it will happen, God's Holy Spirit will come live in your heart.

You will know, your hair won't be shinier, you won't sing any better, physically your appearance won't change at all, but there will be some phenomenal physical things happen. You will get goosebumps all over when God's Spirit moves through you. You will weep uncontrollably sometimes because of the joy that you feel. I have been to some services that I just can't describe accurately with words. I will just say the Holy Spirit, in those times, is the same one that filled believers in the early days. Peter had to explain to the fellow believers on the day of Pentecost two thousand years ago. "Let me explain to you," Peter said. "This is what the prophet Joel has spoken about." That would have drawn the attention of the Pharisees, because they knew what all the prophets had said by heart, and they could not deny what the prophet said.

I am sure there were those in the crowd that said, "Yeah, people have been saying that He is coming for years." Does that sound familiar?

A lot of the very people that were supposed to know the scriptures were arguing with the ones who had seen them fulfilled. Then all at once, the Bible says there was a sound and a wind that came into the area, and all of sudden people of different nationalities were understanding each other's language. By the way, this was the same God that used His Holy Spirit to confuse the people's language in the book of Genesis Chapter Eleven.

That Spirit will now guide you through life if you will just yield to the direction He leads you. That is where the abundant life begins, when you begin to follow the path He has laid out for you. For Janie and me, that meant preforming a miracle to save Dusti from that fish pond. Thank You, God, for that. Our lives have been so much more abundant with her in it.

1. Do you believe in angels?
Yes/no.

Explain your reason

2. Have you ever experienced something that you knew, or at least had the feeling that God must have intervened with to keep you from harm? We like to call these things coincidences. Read Psalm 34:7.

3. Try to remember a time when you were surrounded by the fear of a job loss, a relationship problem, maybe an employee you work with, almost any situation when you were afraid of the upcoming encounter.

Write some notes about your story or stories here. Be prepared for God to use these testimonies to help others.

Chapter Five

Grace is Provision

Scripture: Psalm 23: 4. Even though I walk through the valley of darkness, I will fear no evil, for You are with me. Your rod and Your staff they comfort me.

My parents divorced when I was about thirteen years old. I can't say I remember much about the reason why they were divorcing. I just know I was there when the sheriff's deputy was waiting for my father to arrive home from work. The officer would not allow Dad to go into the house. Dad got to take what clothes mom had packed for him to take with him that night and that was all. As far as I know Dad had no idea this was going to happen. That was a pretty traumatic thing for a twelve year old boy to see.

My father is one of the greatest men that has ever walked on this earth. He never deserved to have this happen to him, but he was able to survive through the ordeal. I remember I had to go to one court proceeding where they put me in this big wooden chair and this guy in a suit said, "Now young man, just who do you want to live with right now?"

I said something that probably broke my earthly father's heart. I could justify my answer, I would have to change schools. I would have to leave my friends. Besides that, he was living with Mammaw Elsie, my grandmother and her husband right now.

I said, "My mom, for now." My words just came out that way, couldn't take it back now. I had decided to take my friends, football, school, and whatever else over my Dad. You can pause to cry here, I did.

Dad and I were fishing buddies, baseball buddies, hunting buddies, and about any kind of thing he could do with me, he would. He taught me so many truths about life that I have tried to pass on to my sons. I wish I had learned how smart he was when I was a young rebel, rather than when I was an old man.

I can remember when I was no more than four years old, I was playing in the back yard and I stepped in a hole that was about as half as deep as I was tall. I ruptured some kind of liner or something and had to go to the hospital for surgery. I remember playing ball in the hall of that hospital with my dad after that surgery.

Before the divorce, Dad had bought a very small Renault car. He had bought a brand new nineteen sixty-eight Chevrolet for a family car a few years earlier. The Renault was his work car and on the top of it we had a rack, so we could put our ten-foot boat on the car when we went fishing. We would go fishing in the local old surface coal mines that the owners allowed to become lakes. Once, when I was about eleven years old, we went fishing to one of our normal spots and the fish were biting so good we waited too late to leave the lake to get back to the car before dark. When we got the boat and the fishing gear loaded up, we headed up the gully filled road we had to take to get back to the main road and it was pitch black dark. We slipped off into one of the tracks that was just too deep for us to get the little car unstuck. I was not much help, too short or too dumb to drive the straight shift. Too small to do much pushing, we were stuck.

About two miles from us was a farmhouse and my dad said, "Son, you are going to have to walk up there to that house and ask that farmer if he can bring his tractor down here and pull the car out while, I stay here and try to dig a path."

I had been to church before, I had heard the Twenty-Third psalm in Sunday School or Vacation Bible School, probably both. This was a scary thing for an eleven year old boy to do. Like I said, it was pitch black dark, no moonlight at all. There were trees hanging over the road, which was more like a trail than a road. I am sure there were all other outdoor noises that are typical on a summer night.

I began to talk to God. I am not sure what I said. I do remember reciting the Twenty-Third Psalm, mixed with the Lord's Prayer or something like that. Something a frightened little boy, who had first met God at a church camp when he was six or seven, would have said.

I walked up to the front door and knocked. After what seem like ten minutes, a light came on inside of the little farm house. I was probably shaking in fear, maybe the people on the inside were too, now that I think about it. Best I remember there was a deep gruffy voice saying, "Who is it?" coming from the other side of the door.

I have no Idea what I said but he let me ride on the tractor fender back down to the car, where he pulled us out and made sure we got back to the main road without hanging up again. I could not take you to that place today, if it even still exists. Even though I was not really walking with God so to say, He was walking with me. The relationship my dad and I had was special for a good while after that night. How could I say, "Mom" on that day after all my father had done with me, he was my best friend.

It seems that for most Christians, their life is a lot like mine was that night back in the middle of nowhere. They know about God, they believe there is a God, but they don't seek Him until they are placed into a place where they have to trust in Him.

The truth is, God is always there. We are the ones who decide who we are going to stay with in life. God wants to be there when you decide on what career to choose. He wants to be there when you marry your spouse. He wants to be there to celebrate with you in your good times and to comfort you when you are sad.

My earthly father is just like that. Every time in our lives, if we needed something, Dad was right there to help us out. It could be a washer or dryer or something for the kids. Any time I was able to build up the courage to ask him, Dad was there to deliver. Now with children of my own, I realize that Dad wanted to do anything he could to help, just like I want to help my children.

God is the same way. We can't be afraid to ask God for the keys to the truck, if we need them. Because just like we would do that for our son, so would God do that for you. Looking back, there were so many blessings that I had chosen to miss out with my earthly father, and there are so many more with my Heavenly One. You don't have to build up courage to ask Him for anything that you will use to glorify the Father.

You will glorify Him when you tell others what He has done in your life and every time He does something that you know only He could have done. His word says in the book of James chapter one verse six, "Pray believing", and when it is fulfilled, shout it from the roof tops to give God the glory.

1. What has been the toughest problem you have had to work through? There are times in our lives when we experience a hurt that feels so bad, we cannot get through it by ourselves.

2. List some places where people seek comfort from? Where did you seek help from your situation, or have you?

3. Are you aware of the fact that God's Holy Spirit will help you through your toughest problems? Read John 14:1-17. This scripture is God's whole plan in a short text message.

Chapter Six

Grace is Guidance

Scripture: Philippians 4:6 Do not be anxious about anything, but in every situation, by prayer and petition, with thanksgiving, present your request to God.

Janie and I became really active in our church and were witnesses to some truly amazing things happening in God's kingdom at that time. We would pray about everything we would do. That didn't happen overnight and unfortunately it didn't last a whole lifetime either.

If you really pay attention to what God is saying to you, then you will be so much happier and less stressed. When Dusti was still a baby, we lived in a nice little two bedroom house that was another miracle story. One day when I got home from work, I was fixing some French fries in the deep fryer for supper and Janie came waltzing into the kitchen. "Guess what we got in the mail today?" she said as she flashed an envelope containing a couple of plastic cards in front of my face.

This was a first for us, we had just become homeowners a little while back, we have a daughter, and now a credit card. One of us suggested we go get one of those new gadgets that lets you watch movies at home, a video cassette recorder. Then, we could stop and rent some movies to watch tonight. What a great idea we agreed, and we zipped out to the car and off to the store we went. After purchasing the machine, we headed back to our house stopping at the convenience store a few blocks from our house. We picked out a couple of new release video cassettes and headed out of the parking lot. We had to yield to two fire trucks pulling out onto the street from the store and we joked, "Hope they are not going to our house."

We followed them right up to our drive way. In my haste to use this new found credit, I had left the deep fryer plugged in and it caught the kitchen on fire. We were out of the house for about two months. It could have been a lot worse. I am not sure why it wasn't; the deep fryer was located in the kitchen, on the center wall of the house. Yet only the kitchen was damaged bad. God had a warning for us about that credit card use that we never learned really well. I think we took the VCR back, but the damage was done. Things like that happen when you do not pray for guidance and follow the direction where the signs lead.

I have a more than a few stories that I could tell you about when Janie and I prayed for a real sign on what our next step should be, and He made it so obvious that we couldn't miss it. The one I am going to share is one of the hardest steps we had ever had to take.

Janie was preschool director in our Sunday School. I was teaching young to medium-aged adults from mid-twenties to forty years old. Our church was growing both in number and spirit. My Sunday School class had grown from six to an average of thirty six. I was beginning to do some lay preaching at small church revivals and filled in on a Sunday once in a while for churches in our area if their pastor was out.

Our church really promoted education for Sunday School growth. Every year some teachers and directors would go on a family vacation to a camp in North Carolina, where they provided leadership training for teachers in the preschool department all the way up to senior adults, as well as outreach administration. It was the closest place to Heaven on Earth that I had ever experienced.

It was that time of year again and we were going with our fellow worshipers and friends to the training retreat for a week. That same time of year was also the time the church nominating committee meets to decide who to ask for the positions the next year. Actually, it was about the last week for those positions to be filled. One of the members on that committee was in my Sunday School class. I called him and asked if they had said anything about asking me to teach again this year, and I mentioned Janie hasn't heard from anyone about her preschool department yet. All he would tell me was they are still meeting.

About six weeks earlier, I had been asked to fill in a Sunday or two at this little church in our town, that a man I worked with attended. We had done a revival there some time earlier and they were waiting on a new pastor to arrive soon and they knew Janie and me from softball and the schools our kids attended. My friend said to me "You and Jeanie, (that is what he called Janie the whole time we served there.) we sure could use your family down at our little church." My family was five, going on six at the time.

They held services every night of the conference. After the service, it was the tradition of our group to get ice cream then meet back at one of the dorm-styled rooms to share our experiences of the day.

I am not sure how many years in a row this has been our family vacation, but this would be the last with this church family.

It was getting later in the week, Janie and I had prayed earnestly about what God wanted us to do. Just give us sign, God, that is all we ask. That doesn't sound like too much does it? God has given signs all throughout time to direct His people. I am not sure how much we believed that He would really give us one. The crowd had filled the place by the time we arrived at the sanctuary for the evening service. We were able to squeeze in a pew that was a couple rows ahead of our friends from home.   Before the service, Janie looked into my eyes and I looked into hers. We asked God once again, "Do You want us to go help out this little church?" I don't know if the preacher was praying or if the choir was singing, I just know it was Janie and me before God almighty.

The service began as a normal service would, with a thousand Christians filled with God's Holy Spirit singing and praising God. Heaven on Earth, as I said earlier. I cannot recall who the lead evangelist was that year, but here is one of those "you know for sure it was God" moments.

When all the pre-service hype was done, the preacher came up to the podium and said, "ladies and gentlemen will you please open your bibles to Isaiah Chapter Six and Verse Eight. The word of the Lord says, "Then I heard the voice of the Lord saying, 'Whom shall I send?' And who will go for us?"

And I said, "Here am I. Send me."

That is what Isaiah said to God when he saw God needed someone to go and tell the people about his amazing grace.

Janie and I looked at each other and hugged as much as we could and sobbed like children for a few minutes. I am sure the people next to us were puzzled or thought we were weird. We knew, we felt that real Holy Spirit directing us on what to do.

When we got back to the room to share our day, Janie and I shared our story with the group. We felt God was calling us to this little church and we would be leaving to join that church upon our return to town. All fifteen of us cried a little bit, like you were sending a relative off to a foreign country.

I know that was God giving us a sign, but there was something else that happened after our fourth child was born. We had been attending the new church for a while now and had gotten as involved as we could with a two year old and a newborn. One morning, when Janie and I went to pick up Daniel, our youngest, the girl working the nursery said she needed to talk to us for a minute.

"Daniel quit breathing for a little bit today. I believe I would have it checked out if I were you," she said.

Janie told me that this girl was a registered nurse and she knew what she was talking about. From that time until Daniel was two years old, he was on a monitor. I sometimes wonder if God was looking ahead to that episode, and because we heeded to His signs, we were in the right place at the right time.

1. Have you ever felt like God was calling you to a different direction in your life? Fell in love, started a new career, moved to a new location are just a few examples.

2. Did you ask God what His plan was for you and then look for an answer? Read Jonah 1:1-3. Have you ever experienced a sign from God and ignored the sign?

3. How do you recognize when it is a sign from God? God will give you direction when you ask Him. If you are praying about something and God sends someone or something into your life, you need to be ready to respond faithfully. Remember, we do not have a coincidental God. Write your experience here.

Chapter Seven

Grace is Doors Opened

Scripture: John 14:13. *And I will do whatever you ask in my name, so that the Father may be glorified in the Son.*

Our God is a Just God. David said in the Twenty Third Psalm that His sheep would have no want. Our second born child, Jon, was five years old and had displayed remarkable skills in baseball. We took him to his school playground to sign up to play T-Ball, which is the very beginning of baseball for children in our area. We were kind of outsiders at the playground. Our kids lived farthest from the school in a neighborhood, and most of the families at the playground were from the rural area.

I don't remember the name of Jon's first coach, but I do remember that he had a son, a daughter, and a niece on the team. Jon was catching fly balls as good as any ten year old in the neighborhood and he was only five years old. We lost every game that year. About three games into the season, I composed a very Christ-like letter to give to the coach explaining how he had a little boy on that team that would help this team win some games if he would just put him in a key position like the other teams did with their best players.

The next game the coach placed Jon inside the white line where the ball becomes dead in T-Ball. That place is where you put the kid that can't pay attention long enough to pick the ball up when it comes in and hand to the dad to put back on the Tee. Janie and I were devastated. We did everything the Christian way. I had felt let down by God, when actually I was being impatient waiting on God. To me, this was a situation that would be detrimental to our son's life. I am sure I said, and probably did, some not so God advised things the next year.

Janie and I had taken ahold of this situation ourselves. We became more involved with the school than with the church. We didn't notice it right away, in fact most teams did not have practice on Wednesday night, much less play games. That night had been set aside for other activities at church or wherever. That was when Jon started baseball, by the time he was done, Janie and I had let almost all of our relationship with God take a seat on the dugout bench. "I am sorry, God."

The next spring when it was time for baseball, Janie and I were worried about the same thing happening to Jon this season and we had been consistently praying about how to handle whatever happened. We arrived at the school for the meeting about baseball that year and we learned that the guy, who coached Jon's team last year, had been transferred in his job to a neighboring county and would no longer be coaching the team. They asked if I would volunteer.

God had done it, He moved the guy to a different county just for us, well, Jon and us. If Janie and I had consulted with God, we would have known better than taking those positions that we had taken with the playground, since God had already cleared the way for Jon to play and display the ability that He had given to him. This would not be the last time God intervened in Jon's baseball career. It would be where Janie and I would begin to drift away from the relationship we had shared with God, that had taken us so far.

Even though God had opened the door for Jon's baseball career, Janie and I were now involved in the secular world more than the church world. Suddenly Wednesday night was ball practice, or a chili supper or anything but fellowship with other believers at our church. When we did have a Wednesday free, we would stay home and enjoy the relaxation. We still played church the best we could, like the Pharisees in Jesus's days. Although we had become involved with the baseball teams throughout the years, we were never the light that God had intended us to be.

Yet, He kept opening doors for Jon throughout his career. When Jon was twelve, God changed the Little League boundaries that had been set for decades to allow Jon to play in another league. That was the just God, and justice did prevail.

Jon was good enough at baseball that if there was a league playing locally, he would be invited to play for a team. The summer before Jon was allowed to play in the city league, he was invited to play in a summer league with a bunch of kids from east county, the city, and the west county. The coach he played for in that summer league drafted Jon in the city league that next year. As I mentioned earlier, this was the first year kids who lived where we lived could play legally in that league. Jon played in both leagues that summer when they did not conflict, when they did, he played in the city.

The year before Jon had made the all-star for the county's team, and it was a real trying experience, probably more so for Janie and me than Jon. The coach of that all-star team's step-son played the same position as Jon, catcher. Although Jon was a better catcher, the coach was married to the other boy's mother. You know what they say, "If momma ain't happy, ain't nobody happy". With that being said, Jon was the backup catcher until God opened a door at the right time. The young man playing catcher whose mom, uh I mean step- dad was coaching the team, got stung by a bee. He danced like his pants were on fire, screaming and trying to get out of his catchers' gear. The boy could not continue in the game, so Jon came off the bench to catch. I am not trying to say that God caused that boy to get bee stung, but a guy that helped the high school coach just happened to be there to watch his son play in the next game. When Jon came off the bench there was a runner on first who had walked. Their coach, thinking our team had to bring in a backup catcher, sent the runner to steal second on the first pitch. When the kid got to second, the ball and the tag were both there waiting. Jon threw out two more runners and had the game winning hit. The coach told us, "Jon sure pulled the team out tonight." Jon didn't play the next night and we lost by the ten run rule and our season was over. However, Jon was the talk of the West County, by the baseball people in the county that had seen him play, including the high school coach he would play for later on.

When the all-star season came the next year, Jon could play in which ever league he chose. At that point, Janie and I were still consulting God on most of our decisions, and trying to teach our children to do so also. We prayed as a family for God to give us a sign and I am sure He did. Jon would not have even got to play in the league or the all-star team if a young man had not had a four wheeler accident. Wild bees and an accident, I'm just saying, God opens doors that you don't know about before you get to them.

Jon's city league all-star team won the state tournament that year. From that point on in Jon's career we went from as far north as Wisconsin and as far west as North Dakota, when Jon was a fifteen year old player in the Babe Ruth league. Earlier, we had traveled with a team that went almost all the way to the east coast to Wilson, North Carolina. Jon played in a world series as a thirteen year old player in the Babe Ruth League. Then, in Jon's senior year in college we traveled as far south as New Orleans, Louisiana. At least Janie and I did, Jon's team had lost their first game in a double elimination tournament in the NAIA world series. We were disappointed, and only a hundred miles or so away from New Orleans, so we went down there just to say we did. Maybe that was being comforted by the world and not by God. We didn't get drunk or gamble lots of money away or anything, but we did not stay behind to be a light to the other parents or players. The opportunity was there, we just ignored the fact we should be sharing our testimony about what all God had done for the last thirteen years to get Jon to where he was today. Some of those miracles were as major in our life as the parting of the Red Sea in Moses's day.

1. Have you ever felt trapped in a situation in which you thought there was no way out? Read John 14:13

2. Who or what do people turn to in those times when you feel trapped? Do you believe that God is concerned about the small things in your life? Can you give an example of when you asked God for a door to open and just like magic, something happened and you realized it had to be God? Read Psalm 25:4

3. List some small things that you should pray about that you didn't realize God really does care about?

Chapter Eight

Grace is Perfect Timing

Scripture; Mathew: 8: 26 He replied, *"You of little faith, why are you so afraid?"* Then He got up and rebuked the wind and the waves, and it was completely calm.

I told you about a story when I was a frightened little boy, this story is about a frightened middle aged man and his wife.

Janie and I had gotten away from our obligations at our little church where we were members, mostly because of baseball travel was the excuse we used. A friend of mine used to tell me "There is a quart of milk in the refrigerator is as good of an excuse as any, if you are trying to justify your actions." To this day, my wife Janie and I quote that to each other when we know we have messed up.

We decided when our two younger boys, Thomas and Daniel, were entering their early teen years, we needed to find something that would hold their interest in a relationship with God. One of the bigger churches in our county had just relocated between where we were attending then and where we lived. They had all the things Janie was looking for and that our family would benefit from, mostly because she liked the music to start with, I think. I am not sure. I am sure why I was there, we covered that earlier about the "momma happy" thing. We began attending regularly and the boys liked the youth leader, so we decided to join the church and get more involved.

We were really excited about our new church and got involved in Vacation Bible School the first summer we were members. Eventually, I began teaching a first grade class with both boys and girls. It was not the first time I had taught young children. As a matter of fact, I had taught the same age group at both of our previous churches.

One Sunday morning at the first church Janie and I joined, I was teaching a lesson on the Holy Spirit, to a group of seven and eight year old children. A mixture of both boys and girls. My assistant was a lady named Barbara. She played guitar and sang the cutest little children songs with such enthusiasm. On that morning, we were sitting around the room on the floor, after singing a song or two, one of the children asked, "How would you know if it was God's Holy Spirit?"

What happened next, you can believe or not, it is your choice, but when you feel those goose pimples, don't quench the spirit. God's Holy Spirit filled that room. I remember the room, it had one window facing west toward the parking lot. All four walls were concrete block and painted light blue. Every one of us in that room that day were filled. We were discussing how the Spirit just came into those people in Acts when all at once, God's Spirit moved through Barbara and me, and we got those goose bumps. One by one, each of those children both felt and saw those goose bumps on their own arms and legs and all over. God did that, just for those children to witness what it was like to be filled. I don't know what they told their parents when they went home that day, but every one of those children were saved by the time they were teenagers.

Sometimes when I was teaching the children in our new church, one of my sons would assist me and he got to know a lot of the children. My youngest son Daniel was the one most involved with the youth group, but still sometimes he would help me with my class. I don't know whether it was working with the children or his relationship with his youth friends, but Daniel was beginning to walk closer with God.

Daniel was working in some kind of children's sport camp going on at church all week during the day. Several of the youth were working the camp playing basketball or something. It was a pretty hot week with temperatures ranging from the low to mid-nineties. At around eleven o'clock that morning our pastor's wife called my cell phone and said something like, "You need to come and get Daniel he is not feeling well," or something.

We only lived about eight minutes from the church, so I headed out the door to get him. Daniel was only fourteen or fifteen at the time, so we were still his transportation most of the time. When I arrived at the church, I waited patiently for a few minutes and remember thinking, come on Daniel hurry up I have to be getting to work soon. I decided that I was going to have to go in and get him, since he wasn't coming out to me. When I walked in the back door to the church Daniel was sitting on a bench type seat with the preacher's wife, Stefanie, and she was asking him questions to check his coherency.

"Do you know who this is?" she asked him as she pointed at me.

I almost fainted! I remember talking to Daniel right away, and I could see a glassy look in his eyes as he replied to her with nothing more than a nod of his head. I called Janie at her work and told her she needed to leave work and get to the church as fast as she could. She only worked about ten minutes away at our local hospital. I went back over to bench where Daniel was still sitting and talked with Stefanie about Daniel. I asked her what happened. She said, "He was refereeing a basketball game outside and said he had to go inside and sit down. When he did, he got all spacey and disoriented." That is when she called me.

I was working at an aluminum factory at the time and part of the training for safety there was about heat exhaustion, heat stroke and limiting one's access to exposure to extreme heat, as well the symptoms of a heat related illness. After observing the conditions of the day and his symptoms, I had concluded that Daniel was suffering from a heat related illness and was probably going to be okay after he cooled off for a while. Janie arrived and came in to the hallway where we were sitting, and Daniel looked up at her. I don't remember if he said anything to her, but you could tell he recognized her. When she asked him if he was ready to go, he kind of nodded and stood up. After two steps he went in to a full blown grand mal seizure. He collapsed to the floor with all the typical movements of someone having a seizure. I called 911 on my cell phone before he hit the floor, while Janie ran into the office to call. By the time the ambulance had arrived, Daniel's seizure had subsided, however he was still a little incoherent.

Before the ambulance arrived, the parents had begun arriving to pick up their children from camp. One of the boys who was in my Sunday School class was at the camp, and his dad was an EMT. He tended to Daniel until the ambulance arrived and even then, he continued to talk to Daniel to keep him calm. They loaded Daniel in the ambulance and headed to the hospital. This was a new beginning for us into the world of Epilepsy.

For the next few years until Daniel graduated high school, Janie and I bonded really close with the youth department in our church. There was not one church youth trip that we didn't take along with youth from that point on. We made a lot of new friends with those children and their parents, some relationships that are still strong today.

I often wonder if that was the main reason God called us to serve in that church. He knew about Daniel before anything happened, and He put us where we needed to be at that time. There were just too many coincidences that happened that were in God's control. I am sure His hand was involved in the timing.

Daniel took medication for seizures for the next few years and then God healed him. Thank you, God.

1. Has God ever intervened in your life at the perfect time? It could be almost anything, flat tire and as you were pulling over to fix it, your friend drove by to help. I am telling you, if you asked God for help and this happens, realize we do not have a coincidental God.

2. Do you trust God? If we follow His direction by praying and then looking for an answer, then He will show us the way. It is when we follow those signs, that sometimes we dismiss as just coincidence, that we will have true happiness in our lives. Read John 10:10

3. List problems that people believe God just can't help with.

4. Is there anything you believe God cannot resolve in your life?   Why?   Read Mathew 19:26

Chapter Nine

Grace is Relentlessly Pursuing

Scripture: Mathew 18: 12&13. 12 *What do you think? If a man owns a hundred sheep, and one of them wanders away, will he not leave the ninety-nine on to the hills and go look for the one who wandered off?* **13** *And if he finds it, truly I tell you he is happier about that one sheep than about the ninety-nine that didn't wander off.*

After my mom and dad divorced when I was younger, God sent someone to live in our neighborhood that was just what I needed. The Thomas family were what you would call meager. They lived in a farm house with a chicken coop in the back yard. This was not in the early nineteen hundred's or something, it was nineteen seventy something. Their house was the only one I knew of around here that didn't have an air conditioner. It was an old farm house that they were living in for very little rent. They would do work when the farmer that owned the house needed them to do something. I think mostly the farmer was a Godly man that recognized the need in their life, just like God saw the need in mine at that time.

Richard Thomas was certainly no saint, but he treated me just like I was his own son. Two of his sons became my best friends. One was in my wedding and I was best man in the other one's wedding. I remember on Saturday mornings the wrestling show would come on their black and white television and we would all gather around to see the action. Before the show was over, we would be Richard's entertainment wrestling in their living room. I never saw him once get mad for the horseplay going on around him. He would laugh and make sure it didn't get too rough and tempers were kept in check.

The Thomas family taught me more about life than any other experiences I have had in my life. They were a quaint, humble couple, raising nine children and me. They never once treated anyone any different, rich or poor. They were not a religious family, they believed in God, but He was not a priority in their lives. They never owned a new car or their own house, but their children never went hungry that I knew about. Both Richard and his wife, Margie, worked in the laundry department of one of our local hospitals until they were unable to because of their health. They got paid on Thursdays and would stop at the grocery on the way home and purchase a weeks' worth of groceries. It would be like ants on an apple going through those groceries to see what special treats they came home with each week. I know now that it was a sacrifice of something nicer, they could have had for themselves. They enjoyed watching us go through the groceries like it was Christmas morning every week.

When I was fifteen, my Mom got remarried and we moved about five miles from the Thomas's house, but I still spent most of my time with their family until they moved to the east end of the county and I could no longer ride my bike over to their new place. I am not sure of the timeline of when all that happened. I know I was thirteen when God put that family into my life and He did it because I needed the love they provided.

Mr. Thomas was somewhat of an amateur farmer. He would raise a big garden and they would can what they didn't eat for the winter. He had animals in the barn lot. The chickens provided eggs for the family, and once in a while, one would be Sunday dinner. He had a pig in the lot at one time, along with two ponies and a horse. He once brought home a turkey, a live turkey. He kept it in the lot until thanksgiving when it was the guest of honor. I was glad to see it gone, I am not sure if I ate any of the bird, but it never chased me across the barnyard any more.

It was the ponies that were the pride of Richard's farm animals. It was the summer weekend events for Richard, his son Donnie, and me. If my Mom had any idea of what was going on there, she would have kept me from going. To her, these people were white trash. To me, they were my sanity. We would load the ponies up in the rickety old trailer, pull them to some small county fairground, and then the fun would begin.

I can't ever remember being with the Thomas family when we won the pony pull, but losing wasn't all that bad when you were having fun all night. It kept my mind off what my home life was like, and the love I experienced with that family is beyond description. Never once did they treat me any different than their own sons, and God knew I needed that.

There was beer drinking, cursing, and some other stuff happening most people would call sinful going on with this group. But God put me there to keep me under His watchful eye. There were a whole lot of worse people out in the world than the Thomas family that I could have hooked up with. You don't understand it when you are going through it because we can't see into the future, but God can. He knew this would be my protection for now. A hurting teenage boy who God loved enough to put a sinner in his life to keep the teenager from being lost. God does work in mysterious ways. I have come to learn as an adult we are all sinners saved by grace. I never really thanked them for what they did in my life, I never realized God had put them there for me, Thank You, God.

This relentless pursuing wasn't just for my protection, it was more of God's plan for the future of the Thomas family. I was saved, and God wasn't pursuing me as much as He was shielding me from a storm. He was pursuing Richard and the Thomas family. After Janie and I got married, we moved to a rental house on Hughes Avenue. We felt like Howard Hughes, in our first place that wasn't an apartment. It wasn't a mansion, either. As a matter of fact, the basement once flooded enough to get up to our washer and dryer. By that time, Mr. and Mrs. Thomas and what children that still lived at home, had moved down the street from where we lived. Their youngest son, Dennis, would come down and play video games with Janie and me. He was probably seven or eight years younger than me and was just like a little brother. Janie and I had become really involved in the church, and we invited Dennis and his brother Bobby to come visit one Sunday. The church at that time was on fire for God. Before long, both of the brothers invited their other brothers. Pretty soon, their parents, started attending, too. The same preacher that led my wife Janie to the Lord, led Richard to the Lord. I was there the Sunday he was baptized. I am not sure about the older siblings of the Thomas family, but the ones I was closest to all got saved. You see, ten years earlier when God put that family in my life to save me from the world, I had no idea what God was planning, but He did. I look back now and see so much of God's hand in that relationship with the Thomas family than I ever realized. Not only did God send a lifeboat for me at thirteen, He was relentlessly pursuing the Thomas family. Richard got to spend the next few years walking with God on earth and I am sure he is walking with God today. Richard passed away when Janie was pregnant with our middle son, whom we named Thomas, after that family.

1. What would you consider walking with God?

   What I want you to see is that this relationship is not a works earned relationship, read Ephesians 2:8-9

2. What are some things that can interrupt your walk with God? Read Mathew 18:12-13. Do you believe when you get too busy in life it affects that relationship you have with God? What does this scripture tell you about how God feels about you during those times?

3. What are some things you can do to strengthen your relationship with God? Read James 2:14-17.

Chapter Ten

Grace is Compassion

Scripture: Psalm 86:15 As a father has compassion on his children, so the Lord has compassion on those who fear him.

Janie and I have been together for almost forty years now and we have both walked close to God, and have wandered from God. He never left us or has forsaken us. There have been many ups and downs throughout our time together as man and wife. We have cried a lot together and we have laughed a lot together, most importantly we have shared our walk with each other with God. There are times when we prayed for something and God opened the door immediately, while other times He knew what we needed before we had to ask. He has never let us go hungry, always kept a roof over our head, and provided a very comfortable life for Janie and me. Why would a God that has the power to create a whole new universe be concerned about two lowly sinners saved by grace? I can't answer the question any other way but with a question. Who among us would not give to their children or would not do anything for their children? That is what we are, a child of God. He is real and if you let Him into your life, then you will experience His grace.

The last story about God I will leave with you is about how amazing it is to have a God that hears your voice, knows your hurts, and will have compassion on you when the time calls for it. Janie and I had a dog when we moved to our first house that we bought. The dog's name was Tobi after one of my wife's favorite ballplayers. His name was Dave Tobik, so she named her dog Tobi. She had Tobi before we met, and I don't think the dog ever forgave me for taking Janie from him. Once that we had a place of our own, we brought Tobi back to our place to live with us. We were still in our twenties and starting on the path God had laid out for us. Tobi was probably fine, but Janie thought he was lonely, so we went to the local shelter and adopted our next dog who we named Sassy, I don't remember why. Back then you didn't get dogs that were spayed already, and we saw no sense in that, besides, a hundred bucks was a hundred bucks. Needless to say, the first time that Sassy came in heat, Tobi fathered her first litter of pups. "Oh, we have to keep one," Janie said, and we did. We kept a girl puppy, Tubby, she was the fattest of the litter, for ourselves. Now we had three dogs, but not for long.

When I came home from work one evening Janie met me at the door with tears in her eyes. She said something is wrong with Tobi. I went outside, and he could hardly stand up, much less walk. Now I want you to understand this was Janie's best friend until I came along. It even hurts now to think about the pain Janie was going through. We took Tobi to the vet and the decision to have him put to sleep was made by both us and the vet. When we left that office after saying good bye to our dog, I told Janie we would never do that again.

When Janie became pregnant for the third time, we began to look for a bigger house and, just like always God pitched in to help. The real estate market was in the tank at the time; Interest rates were up and the demand for houses was a lot less than the availability of houses. When we sat down at the kitchen table of the home we live in now, we looked out the window to see our daughter Dusti, almost three, playing in the back yard like it was her place already. The realtor told us not to expect anything too soon, because of the slow market, not wanting to get our expectations up too high.

While sitting there at the kitchen table we asked the realtor if she believed in God. She kind of blew us off with a casual, "Oh sure." We were studying the Gospel of John at the time. Just a side note, read the Gospel of John once a year. It is full of promises from God to us. One of those promises was anything you ask for in My name to glorify the Father you will receive. No ifs, no ands, and no buts, that is what it says. Look it up for yourself right now, John 14:13. We shared that scripture with her and told her we believed with all our heart that God would provide for us to get this house. It was less than two weeks later, and our house sold, and we began the closing on our new house.

Our two dogs, Tubby and Sassy went with us to the new house. Eventually, they got out of the back yard. Sassy was the only one that came home. On her way home from work, Janie passed a dog on the side of the road and it looked like our dog. I went up to where Janie saw her, and I took an old sheet, wrapped her up in the sheet, and took care of the situation as best I could. I am sure we cried, although I don't remember it as much as some other times when we were sad. After Sassy passed, we were dog-less for a while. We were raising children now, so the concern was more on their activities than anything else at that time. We were still walking with God pretty close, because we had not yet gotten to the point where the secular world would try to steal us from God.

I don't know for sure how long it was before we became dog owners again, but I have always loved dogs and so has she. I believe God put those kinds of pets here not only for our companionship, but to help us to learn to deal with losses in our life.

Right after my mom and dad divorced a man, and his wife moved in next door to where we lived. They had two German Shepard puppies. This is another one of those God stories that you might see on a Hallmark special on television. One of the puppies adopted me. There was a chain link fence between our house and the Craig's house, and every day that puppy would be waiting for me to either come home from school, or come outside in the morning on non-school days. His name was Rex and he was my best friend when I needed one. As Rex grew older, he learned to scale the fence between our yards, and now, instead of waiting for me on his side of the fence, he would be waiting for me on our side. This did not please my mom or Mr. Craig in the least bit. They could not stop him, that dog's love for me was supernatural.

The Craig family moving away hurt more at that time than my parents' divorce. Rex was still their dog. They moved to a small community about five or six miles from where we lived, and Rex was gone. I am sure I cried, I was only thirteen years old. I would cry today, too. Two days later when I came home from school, there was Rex sitting on our front porch. I don't know what goes on in a dog's mind, and neither does anyone else but God. I can tell you for sure his emotions, as well as mine. He was as glad to see me as I was to see him.

Mom took Rex back to the Craig's once more, then Rex came back to our house. This time Mr. Craig told my Mom, "That dog loves your son more than us. Let him keep the dog." Rex came back from the Stanley community twice then Mom gave him to a family that lived thirty miles from our house, to a town named Lewisport. Two weeks later, Rex was right there on my porch again. Mom took him back one more time and again Rex started home, but he never made it back that time. I don't know what happened to Rex, but I do know if there are dogs in heaven, when I get home, Rex will be sitting on my porch waiting for me to get there.

Once we got another dog, we kept dogs in and around our house, even up to the writing of this book. The "compassion" this chapter is titled for comes from a story about one of these dogs. Daisy was her name. We got her when she was just a puppy. I think some girl Janie worked with had a litter of puppies to get rid of and Janie was willing to take one home. Daisy was a one of a kind breed some would call a mutt. She had the body of a Labrador retriever, but the legs of a dachshund. She had a great personality, loving, and almost too clingy sometime. Her biggest flaw was that if she got a chance to get out of the yard, zip right across the field she would go. I would get so mad, I couldn't see straight. I would yell her name, whistle, everything I could do, but she would just keep running. After an hour or so, she would come home and sit by the front door wanting to come in the house. God taught me a good lesson with her and I even wrote a sermon about her called "When Daisy Comes Home." Once, after one of these episodes of running, I realized that Daisy and I were a lot alike. When God called me to do something for Him, I would run away just like her. Then eventually, I would return to front door hoping God would let me back in the house. He always did. Thank You, God.

When Daisy got older, she was barely getting around the house and struggling to breathe. Never once did she act like she was in any pain or suffering at all, she was still too clingy sometimes. Janie and I had discussed taking her to the vet and having her put to sleep, but she wasn't suffering that we could tell. I made the decision that the next Monday morning when I finished my weekly round of golf, I would take her to the vet. That would be easier for Janie, I thought. I went in to work my afternoon shift on Sunday with this laying heavy on my mind. It would still be a painful loss for both of us and I was not sure that would be the way Janie wanted to say goodbye to Daisy.

I live forty five minutes from where I work and as soon as I left work that night I began talking to God. "I can't do this God, I can't take one of my best friends to die." I cried like a five year old while I talked to God. I mean I was talking out loud in my little car to the Creator of the universe and crying like a child. When I got home, I told Janie what my plan had been, to take Daisy in the morning so she wouldn't have to be there, but I just couldn't do it. Janie fed the dogs like any other night, while I was doing something with my keyboard in the kitchen. I saw Daisy get a drink of water before waddling on in to the living room, where Janie had made her a place where she could rest more comfortably. After about fifteen minutes, Janie yelled in to the kitchen "Daisy just died." We hugged, we cried, then we did what had to be done. I just want to point out to you here that with over six billion people on this planet, God heard the prayer of a sixty-year-old man who was about to lose a dog, and He cared enough about me to have the compassion to save me from the brunt of that hurt. Oh, it still hurt, but I knew it was God's grace being done just for me.

1.What does compassion mean to you?

2. Has there ever been a time in your life that you knew it was God's Holy Spirit that comforted you? Read Matthew 14:13-14. Even in a time of great sorrow for Jesus, He saw the needs of others and He gave them compassion.

3. How can you know that God's Holy Spirit helps you with compassion when, you are in need? Read Luke 11:11-13. Can you share a time when you prayed for compassion and something miraculously happened that you attributed to just coincidence? Always remember, we do not have a coincidental God.

Grace Times Ten Closing Thoughts

Scripture: Matthew 28:20b. *Lo, I am with you always until the end of the world.*

These are just a few stories that I have shared about experiencing God's total grace. My prayer is for you to take these verses and write your own testimony of God's grace in your life. Not just these ten scriptures, but any scripture that God has used to show you His amazing grace. Take your miracle stories and share them with your children and your children's children, so they too may experience God's complete grace. I hope this book has helped you see all that God has for you.

One of the main purposes in writing this book has been to hopefully help you to be able to reflect on all of your own personal experiences of God's grace, and you are now more prepared to share your personal testimonies. Every Christian has a personal testimony that he or she can share with others who may need God's grace in their own life. Will you consider sharing, so more people can experience His grace?

In addition, it is also hoped that you will become more aware of your own personal experiences of God's grace as they are happening now. God will bless you and you will see the Holy Spirit at work in your life when you trust in Him.